# We Are All Wildflowers

A Poetry Collection

# Britt Matthews

To request permissions, contact at info@fringedbluestar.net
Paperback: ISBN: 979-8-9900210-2-0
Second paperback edition September 2024.
Cover Art by Christon Anderson
Art Photography by Michael Booini
Interior Layout & Cover Design by Dennis Layden
Back Cover Photography by Louis Columbus

"When a flower grows wild, it can always survive
Wildflowers don't care where they grow."
-Dolly Parton

To my mother, Karen Key Smith for fan-girling over my first poem about seagulls I penned as a seven year old at Hutchison Beach Elementary.

To all the teachers, that worked day in and day out and took the time to encourage me. Your job is thankless at times, but you made a difference.

To Angie Thompson, an old family friend and fellow creative that has been my fairy godmother for years.

To Martha Foy, for her gentle nudging and common love of flowers.

To my children, Jack and Piper for their love and support.

Dear Reader

To see and be seen, is the most beautiful dance of humanity.....and I hope you will dance with me.

It is my hope that through my writing I will help people feel seen. Sometimes I don't feel like my words are my words but I am just merely a conduit for a force greater than myself. I have felt that same kind of warm blast to the soul when I have read words that have moved me over the years.

Joyce Kilmer's "Trees" was the first poem I remember being captivated by and I find myself routinely drawn to those writers that had a spiritual connection with the natural world; it felt like "church" to me.

The premise of this poetry book "We Are All Wildflowers" was inspired by the natural tenacity of wildflowers. I think people are a lot like wildflowers, so many of us have been tossed aside for "weeds" but in actuality we can survive, and even thrive despite harsh conditions.

I want to give others the feeling I get when I read Mary Oliver's "Wild Geese", the way it hugs you and all your messy bits and seems to say… you are beautiful just as you are.

I want to make people feel seen, the way I felt as a young teen when I read "Harlem" by Langston Hughes for the first time.

I choose to believe that each and every one of us have something to share and there are people in this world waiting to hear those exact things and THAT is all part of the dance of seeing and being seen.

Love your way
Britt

# Contents

# Yes, I am A Wildflower

Yes, I am a wildflower
the kind that you can't help but trip on
when you are running down the path
the kind that tickles your ankles
when you're having a laugh
the kind whose color
reminds you of something beautiful
but you can't recall
A warm memory
somewhere between winter and fall
I grow off the grid
and can take the stomping of boots
of passers through
explorers and even suits
looking for bigger things
like cash flows and cap rates
and more evergreen
but as soon as I am picked
I fall to the floor
my color bright
No more.

# Taking in Water

What is a flower before she blooms?
Resilience rising
Hope conspiring
Breathing life, however turbulent
into the seeds
Taking in water and
Turning thoughts into things.

# In Season

Whatever is blooming
whatever is coming to life
that is the flower
upon my spirit wishes
to catch a ride.
I like to think that
every fragrant petal
and showy stem
floating in the wind
is praising God
part of nature's hymn.

I like to ponder that the people
that have left this earth
are breathing life and wonder
through the anthers and the seed
and coming back to me
in moments sweet
like the first bloom of Spring.

# Let Me Swing Back

I want to know the peace you can set a clock to
a balance restored
that can't be ignored
like Galileo found in the swinging lamp at church when he was bored
I want to feel my true center
the kind that leaves you floating
after a good family dinner
that makes Descarte proud
where you can dream and drink
and rise above the laughter aloud
God, if you are there
Let me swing back, back to you.
No matter where I am,
Let me swing back, back to you.
I'm wise enough now to let nature be my proof
Let me swing back, back to you.
I want to know the stillness
no matter the weight pulling me to and fro
over all of the stones
engraved with truths they insist I should know
They want us standing up and shaking it out
like a rock concert is breaking out
but they also want us seated, kneaded and kneeled
but then speaking in tongues and showing we are healed
How do I keep up with my lines?
Is that where I am supposed to be?
I didn't think there would be so many rules
to living free
I want to know the grounding
I had in the middle of the storm
where there were no walls or halls
to keep us quenched and warm
I didn't need a building to access you before
not sure why I think I need it now
except maybe it gets lonely
trying to figure it all out.

# The Truth is Easy to Tell

The truth is easy to tell
It is our shame
that gets caught
in our throats.
A phlegm trail of fear
we find impossible to clear
until we get the boys
or the steroids
or whatever we need
to open us up
and breathe again.
The truth is easy to tell
It is there waiting on the ledge
of the wishing well
ready to grant you
your freedom.
If you have the courage
to wait for the copper to clink
don't wait too long
don't try so hard to think
The truth is easy to tell.

# Grit to Groan

Groin to grommet
and I couldn't stop it
looking for ways to be held
before you turned from griffin to gelded
to GOAT again
Grit to groan
you dropped me off at a place
that wasn't home
At first I thought it was a hard flush
there was a card
you didn't touch
so the metal didn't make
the mix Into the flux
and so steadfast
my gristle whistled In the wind
running fast until my muscle's end
and while gravity grazed me
It couldn't take me all the way down
so I floated while you gloated at the flywheel
ss I fell asleep to the film reel
so put your grievances on the griddle
and fry them up fast
while you can stand the smoke
that soils your clothes fast.

# Gum Tree

I need all of the sun
and the joy of a cheetah in a full run
I burn easy and red
my blood for you
to dye your sweats or you skin
none of us like the box
we are living in.

# They Do Not Move

They do not move they say
because they don't know
they don't know
as the water ebbs and flows
so do the cells inside of us
moving so slowly
or sometimes quickly
their hubris misses
our hydraulic mastery.
How laughable it is to say
that bloom doesn't move
because your eyes don't catch
the way their leaves dance
because you have
no way to measure
a circumstance
beyond your own understanding.

# Me Too

Two words
Is this a game
like charades?
where I put my fingers up
and my shame down and hope that
you will understand me, no, believe me
for the win?
Two words
One space
deep and cavernous
neverending
hope and confusion pending
Two words
Five letters
are not enough
and yet
they feel
like too much.
So I pause
I pause long and hard
Is this worth letting down my guard?
Do I stand up for something
or be quiet
and feel EVERYTHING
Again.
How is that a win?
I stare at my keyboard
Wondering who will make the first move
Will it do any GOOD?
Am I just a pawn in this game of distraction?
Will in fact this trend, this hashtag, offer any traction?
Two words
Five letters
Once I pull the trigger,it is there forever
Not enough
Too much
Good girls
don't make a fuss.

# Crown Yourself

You do not need permission
from your spouse, your lover
your child, your mother
Or any other person other
than you
Crown Yourself
You have all you need
to do what you want
as soon as you let go
of your need to please
You will see the fruit
of your prophecy
Crown Yourself
No one is coming to place
the gold on your head
they are hunting their own jewels
let us not confuse
the desires of others as our own
Crown Yourself
take it out of the glass case
TODAY
there is no reason to wait
You have spent far too long
letting yourself down
take a breath and put on your
Damn
Crown.

# Fear is a Fickle Weasel

Fear is a fickle weasel
scurrying and jumping
knocking over the easel
where our dreams are painted
some good
some bad
but always wrapped
in what we "could have' had.

Fear is a slippery fish
that doesn't want to be caught
but we throw out the line anyway
despite what we have been taught.

She loves to tease you
and others in your boat
distancing you from the ones you love most.

The more illusive
the more grand a catch she is
Fear is a slippery fish.

# Motion

We seem to be moving still
but we are actually moving
that is the line that threw me
off my axis in just the right way
I fell out of my center
and down the looking glass
and saw treasure where I once smelled trash.
I pondered the truth as I was floating
through my ego's clatter and the gray matter
of thousands of hearts before me
My love ancestry?
I felt their hope and pain at once
like tendons on fire after a day of rain
heroes now, but they died heretics
fervently unapologetic
about a world they could not explain
but knew wasn't flat
and surely wasn't still.
No matter how bloody the threat
or how low the till
they kept counting
the hope coins in their pocket
adding up the beauty
on God's number line
on which I count
while I am floating
with the rest of the dreams on legs
they take for granted
I shall keep moving
No matter how I am branded.

# Your Jesus and Mine

I wonder what they would talk about
if your Jesus and mine
sat down for a bite…..
Would they munch on crudites or french fries
or open your grandmother's wine?
Would they get all beginning of time
on each other
Eden and sin
and the fall of the first mother?
or would they get coptic
giggling, whispering
sweet gnostics
before they buried it all
In politics?

# Cufflinks

Form and function
showed up at the same talk
met metal and stone and glass
Hey! Let's go for a walk
I like your style
I like your class
You here to hold up shirts?
Me too!
Want to stay for dessert?
we can commiserate
our master always running late
grabbing us rough
not enough love.
We can deliberate over
Kissing cuffs and those vulgar
barrel ones
What are we going to do
When all the artists die?
and we are all left in the drawer....
Will we be beautiful anymore?

# Peter's Child

I tried to walk on water
but my faith did not hold.
My feet felt the weight
and I was no longer bold.

He asked me, why did I doubt?
I wanted to confess
that is how I am wired.
I've always traversed on land
and believing in something new
can make you quite tired.

# Dirty as a Stove

Dirty as a stove we never cleaned
until it was moving day, and we needed
the deposit for the baby's milk
Dirty as a stove that saw fires and lies
and the back of mama's thighs
when she heard yellin' in the other room
it will all be over soon.
Dirty as a stove drippin' with plantain grease
frozen pizza
and old pig's feet
times were never good, on the days we would meet.
I learned to connect the shining with the leaving
the fumes with not breathing
exhaustion with completion
maybe that's why I never quite seem
to finish a task?
How do I feel?
Dirty as a stove
if you stop to ask.

# The Moon is Mad Again

The Moon is Mad Again
and I can't blame her
with all the world
trying to tame her.

The earth is flat again
because not one wants to play catch
with a ball
they can't carry.
They are tired from all the spinning
so they hired a judge to say they're winning
and decided
the earth is flat
and the moon
is mad.

# When It's All Said And Done

When it's all said and done
we will hot glue the masks together
craft time makes it better
like garland for the next baby shower
Do we have those anymore?
When it's all said and done
we will move on to the next story
they pushed into first place
and forget about the tragedy
that's happening
right in front of our face.
When it's all said and done
we will move and deal
by sharing a snarky meme
while others try to heal
and wonder what we mean.
When it's all said and done,
I will wonder what kind of havoc awaits
in my little girl's chest
Did I make the right choice?
Did I do my best?

# Hindwing Tails

Mmm....
Another American
Sweet Gum
Yum....our friends say,
we can drink you under the table
any day.
Give me all the juglone
your walnuts and hickories give me such delight
Why do you put up such a fight?
I won't hurt them and they won't hurt me
what's poison to the rest, is poetry to me
you would know if you followed the INSTA
of the famous London apothecary
who finally SAW me
Oh, James.
Thousands of years I roamed
together and alone
and finally they landed on a name
but they kept changing it until
they found something that suited them
Nevermind me.
They say I have two weeks to live
but I fly above clock hands
and your checkbox plans
my heart is nocturnal
and your limitations diurnal
so we find ourselves at an impasse.
Ssssh, there is a bat.
Oh good, my wings evaded the
bastards again.
I can't fit into my pants
but they help me dance
and keep the predators away
Do you think you will love
your hindwing tails some day?

# Sunshine

It's hard to conjure up unrest
when I am reaching
for papas fritas
and feeling my best
walking to the laundry
across the parking lot
doesn't matter where
I am going
Sunshine makes my hips
Extra hot.
Looking for some conflict
to stir up some soul wit
but I can't seem to find it
so I will scribble while I wiggle
This happy
Feeling
like it has to be wrong.
so I clench while I resist
until I hear my favorite song
going to turn it up
soak it up
Sunshine
never stays too long.

# Painting my Nails

One of the only times
I am still
and I can bend
the colors of my life
to my will.
They are both loud and quiet
with the bright sheen
of possibilities
not yet seen.
The lime green dress
that turned heads
on a night
meant for equations
Not teenage palpitations.
The pale mauve
meant for polite conservations
at a bridal shower
that ungodly hour
when I pretend to care
about lawn furniture
and prepaid vacations.
The extra hot coral
straight from a street mural
and the bottom
of that old bikini
I wish I had never thrown out
so much to dream about
when I am painting my nails.

# Home

You are worn leather
and all at once, fresh sheets
A favorite song that acquires
more magic on repeat.
You are warm biscuits
and my mama's favorite Sunday hymn
A sweatshirt from college
with holes that will never be filled
a rainy afternoon that invites me
to be still.

You are jumpin' in the waves
on the last day of school
my grandmothers' box fan
keepin' us cool
when the heat and the flies
won't leave us alone
You are sleepin' in
You are home.

# Falling Back in Love

It has not been a reunion
Ravenous
like we were caught in the closet
just the two of us
I did not run and jump to meet you
across the pavement with you swinging me around
It's been a gradual courtship
a tune here
a tune there
gentle reminders that
my voice had gone nowhere
except to make a deal
in a backroom with my fear
but I am waiting to meet her
and tell her I need her here
right beside me
to bring light in me
to help me feel the fight in me
the drive in me
I need her to ride with me.

# Regret

The funny thing about her
you wouldn't know it's her
when you cross her path
because she's kind and cunning
and happy to make you laugh.
A dream tickling, shape shifting siren
that you will not recognize
for no one willingly, swallows lies.
She is the butterfly that flew over you in the park
that you did not stop to admire
She is the chocolate truffle with sea salt
you dared not desire
the young man selling popcorn you did not require
She is the grandmother you never took the time to know
the niece that begged you to join her in the snow
the former flame that you never let go.
She's present everywhere
but only
if you let her in.
Let her knock on someone else's door
you have adventures to begin.

# Cheetah

Since the moon drew me in
I've been eyeing this steel
So I find their measuring sticks
a little unreal.
I don't remember anyone asking me
If I would be content with fourteen feet
or If I would even want packaged meat?
It's embarrassing
but all I can do is wait.

I don't need a new master
just a new moment
I don't need to bend the steel
I just need a little wind
so the balance wheel
tips her hat in my direction
don't need the priest
to make my confession.

That little girl that eyed me earlier today
she's got the moon in her bones
and I could feel her night
All day.
We had a conversation her mama didn't hear
seems we are both waiting
for the path to be clear
so we can
Run
Run
Run.

# Shutdown

It's so unbecoming
to see all the running
It's all too rhythmic
this pandemic
I think I speak for us all when I say
Why can't you just get with it?
Put your Evian down
Stop blaming and start bridging won't you?
Stop hitting and start fitting
the pieces together
before they dissolve into forever.
I promise you would find
the burden lighter
if you would just whisper to your inner fighter
Psst!
Ego and and agreement are hard to carry
in the same hands
So could you turn around?
Put your designer gloves down
a hold on your travel plans
and consider a solution?
We feel your heavy and sweaty
Dissolution
All the confusion
You guys forgot
you're out of shape
you're out of breath
and yet you can't confess
You still really want to fit
in that party dress.

# Addiction

The quiche is in the oven
and I'm thinking about your lovin'
and wishing it wasn't
so insidious
Rosemary is weary
with all the ones that love me
for they too are curious
and furious all the same.
Here I am again
slow motion dying
laughing and crying
at once
but no one
wants to make a fuss.
So we pretend
the tissues are sashes
we use to keep
our party dresses on
pretty and taught and tight
like a youthful forehead
we all want.

# Show the Work

Show the work
scribble the numbers
in the margins or down the sides
it doesn't matter
we know messy things
come from beautiful minds.
And so I find myself asking
from you the same..
Show the work
Show me how you added all these things up
smiling and nodding
is not enough.

# How Smart I Was

How smart I was
when I knew everything
exactly how to place it
neatly In boxes and rows.

How smart I was
when I could dive into the facts and the stats
and the stories that promised
all the things that mattered
before my ideas were shattered.

Before I realized life
was a book with the pages missing
with mold in the spine
both messy and divine.

# Ride

I bet we are learning a lot
about ourselves right now
he said
and I felt egos' wind rush out
and the emptiness that wants to know
really know what we are made of
when we don't turn to numb
ourselves from the chaos.
God
take me home
to my center
until there are no more atoms to divide.
I don't have to know
nor do I have to understand
anything but
the fact
that noone
can swim on dry land.

# Roll Up Your Sleeves

Roll up your sleeves
I'll loosen my tie
We'll dig up some dreams
and throw them in the sky
and watch it rain
and dance in the puddles
until we feel no pain.

Roll up your sleeves
I'll take off my belt
We'll move what we can
put the rest on the shelf.
I don't need your answers
I don't need your lies
I don't need your glory
and I don't need your sighs.

Roll up your sleeves
before we say our goodbyes
Roll up your sleeves
I'll put my drink down
wipe off my brow
and let you wear my crown
and we will reign
and dance in the diamonds
until the son comes down.

# Satin Gloves

She wanted flowers
it never occurred to her
not to put them
in her own cart.
Lilies or lilacs violets or  roses
whatever her heart supposes
she threw them in with gusto and I
thought we must go
to this place, more!
I thought of my satin gloves and
fine china
eating sundaes just because at your
favorite diner
the "good" towels
and the lacy things
with the tags still intact
Why do we work so hard
to live in the lack?
Surely
I don't want to be  teaching
my children this???
Jesus-Others-You
I remember the poster
and the ghost of her
that girl inside me
that rattled me with shame
You are last, you are last
all in his name??
But am I convinced
partly from living
and partly from sense
that, surely is not what he  meant.
Love your Neighbor
as you love yourself
was just the Golden Rule said

in a different way
not an invitation
to throw ourselves away
or put ourselves last.
Love does not run out
when we
take a helping first
it just gets
the giving train going
and puts
your satin gloves to work.

# Athena

Athena or Aphrodite
They both are, a different kind
of mighty
when they come
to the right  party
with the right quiver
knowing just what tricks
what kicks, to deliver.
First she must
open the door
and survey around
Is it safe
to let her armor down?
So the hour strikes
and the owl flies
For he can't
perch on her braids
Nor can he sit idly by.
Be strong
Be courageous
but first, sweet, delicious.
Peel back the outrageous
with your faith
with your  love
But still, be strong
be courageous
Because you don't know
which river is your Jordan
And so every time
we get wet
we are prepared
for the depths.
Because we don't know
which battle is our Jericho
And so every time

we walk
Waiting for the next round
the chord change
our cue
to pack away our gown
or let our hair down.

# You Matter

When someone writes Black Lives Matter
and you feel the hair on your skin rise
Please
ask yourself, WHY?
Are you afraid there is something in you
that they are trying to deny?
When they declare a certain group worthy of affection
why do we take it to mean
the others didn't quite make the selection?
When did we become a world of one way or another?
Are we not each other's sister, each other's brother?
Why are we using us and them
when "we" will do just fine?
Something to think about
when we share online.
When someone writes Blue Lives Matter
and you want to share a story of brutality
take a moment to think of all the times
that shade protected you and me.
Ask yourself
why you are so quick to refute worth and affirmation
perhaps it is you
struggling
with your own self condemnation?
When someone tags All Lives Matter
consider it not
An affront
to your own circumstance
they are struggling for meaning
just like you, they so badly want to express
Don't you think they deserve that chance?
If we would take a minute to listen
we would hear
a bunch of children of God
just dying to know they matter.
You
Matter.

# Shadow Calling

I have a shadow calling
and he's out hauling
all the things I care about like the evening's trash
and I can't seem to pack that away.
I have a shadow calling
and she's out rehearsing lines I'll never write
in someone else's play.
I have a shadow calling
and he's always
adding items
to my list
with golden stars
and lines that always
seem to fit.
I have a shadow calling
and she's always
Purring, *Darling*
inviting me to come along
take a seat
and drink my sweet
How could I be wrong?

# Sitting in Your Chair

Sitting in your chair
hoping for magic
smiling at the cat scratches
damage others might find
tragic
though I feel the little rifts
in leather
are gifts
reminding us
there is nothing
better
than the hold
of memory
she is warm and fragrant
and safe
like a grandmother's hug
after a really long day
Sitting in your chair
praying, today
as we run into others
also walking home
we leave our wounds
alone,
let us be kind,
and aware, and remember
there is always a story
behind every tear.

# My Favorite Number is a Color

What if flowers had no color
and birds had no wings
the moon had no song
and people only dreamt of things?
What a miserable world
with only black and white
harsh lines
and no delight.

Is that the price we pay
in the name of being right?

# I've Hit My Knees

I've hit my knees
against the excuses I have made
and I've traded secrets
with the games we have played
and cried out
cried out
Lord, please haven't we paid enough?
My soul wallet's empty
and yet my karmic debt
seems to still
be racking up.
I've hit my knees
against the altar
and asked God to take my anger
only to pick it up again after
there were no traces of
that little magic wafer.
But I know no matter how
hard I run
Grace will always catch up to me
and so I left
the getaway plane at the hangar
and cried out
Lord!
Don't let my doubt
get the best of me.

# Begging

Hypnos
I begged for you to come
but you never came.
Every toss
Every turn
Every slow burn
of a vision
that Morpheus
never blessed
in sober sheets
I would have never guessed
you wouldn't cover me.
A puzzle piece I couldn't solve
a wayward violin that wouldn't resolve
or finish the thought
she had on her lips
Hypnos you offered your hand
but I wanted your kiss.

# Happy

They all have that same look
eyes squinted
forehead scrunched
shoulders hunched forward
so they can hear you better
as if to clarify
Why?
What do YOU have to be sad about?
And so the mini trial begins
you must decide what to present
or hope they forget
they ever saw your lament.
Surely their concern
Is supposed to be relieving
but their not believing
not even conceiving
the shade of blue you see the world in
hurts more than the moment
before they knew, when all was good
and the masks behaved as they should.
Their discomfort climbs
under your skin
puts your hair on end
whispering to you, It is better to pretend.
And so you do
because that's what it seems
they want from you.
So you can imagine
how sweet it is when someone walks along
and listens with eyes soft
head tilted and shoulders, relaxed
listening not with their fear
but to the facts
like just because it's easy to cry
doesn't mean
you don't love to laugh.

# Debutante

My ideas are on the edges of the ballroom
eager like the ladies waiting to be picked
who have raced the clock rehearsing
while the candle chased the wick
for a dance my mama taught me accidentally
and my daddy never knew
to be smart is a clever secret
you may not share, nor declare
with more than a few.
Standing still I felt the swaying, hoping
their lines are smooth
like the satin on these dresses
I hope their ribbons prove
to be perfect for the tresses
their mothers teased just right.
So much made ado
about this night.
Don't they know?
It's not their fine gloves
that send us blushing
but just the right questions
will get us gushing
well past the waltz
and any faults of yours or mine
my brain would love
a dance this time.

# Paradox

I have lost all the things
I have clutched too tight
and found all that I have been willing
to surrender to the night
I have lost the patience
that endured small talk over cocktails
and the illusion of balance
that had me gawking at handrails.

I have lost a butterfly shaped gland
and the chemicals her wings spread
and gained an appreciation for life
full hair and fuzzy socks instead.

I have lost what could have been
and carried the grief way too long
found and re-found the truth
that comes with singing one's song
I have lost the desire
to argue with people I do not esteem
and found that we are all just treading water
in the same survival dream.

# Wonder

I could feel anger rising
and I knew that was the bell tiding
my soul reminding me
how stretchy a fabric
mercy really is
how it covers us all
and ails us of our fits.
I kept recounting
that girl that told of the Sikh
and the magic he found
at the top of the peak
when you are tempted to hate
You must wonder instead.
You must wonder
when it's the last thing you want to do
the last place you want to visit
You must wonder
because it is healing's prerequisite.
You must wonder
when you listen
when you think
when you speak.

# Hallelujah Anyway

The clothes are in piles
And the No's are running miles
around the mail you haven't opened
Hallelujah anyway
I promise there is peace on a porch
just past all the commotion.

The towels are heavy and dirty
and the knots in your stomach swirly
with no milk in sight
Hallelujah anyway
I promise there are warm gusts
waiting to dry your skin
and soothe your musts.

The wolves are hungry
while worry feasts on the lawn
listening to the music
while you look for gifts
to pawn
Hallelujah anyway
I promise there is relief
that will come.

# Dragonflies

Some of us metamorphosize In
front of each other's eyes
Oh, you have lost weight!
or congrats on this or that
But others need a while
to transition to breathing air
to change under the water
like nymphs that hate to bother
others with their crackling shell
It's noise, it's messy bits
so we stay under the depths
and wait for our time to rise
So don't discount the wings
you can't' see
they are in fact
fluttering, and waiting, gently
Will you wait with me?
and so we grow uneven
Anisos
Learning more as the story goes
our hindwings are broader and
bolder
than what we have before us
Isn't that the way it always is?
Isn't that wisdom's promise?
But if you are in the dark, so am I
So are we, all, under the water
hopefully, growing stronger
So we can be brilliant and
iridescent
With whatever time we have left
And see, we must, in all directions
As we ascend and transcend From
the depths
though deep and dirty, necessary
And soul worthy.

Come fly with me
And we will pass
The damselflies
And join
The dragonflies.

# I Would Like To

I would like to
do six impossible things
before breakfast
and high five everyone
that understood this
I would like to
dissolve the world's angst
on my lobster telephone
and always have Gilbran
whispering in my home.
I would like to
have pet dragonflies
sing my favorite songs
and be in love with my thighs
and at peace with my wrongs
I would like to
love and love and love
until my heart can't anymore
and always tell the hurting
my office, has an open door.
I would like to help others
find their highest selves
but I know, I must
tackle me first
and silence the voice
that negotiates my worth.
I would like to
be the person
my soul deserves.

# Uncaught

The rings are scarred
and their confidence marred
by the moths and butterflies
that overcame
and flew past the obstacles
and left their scales
to be washed away
to prepare for a new dawning
they embark
sing with wings yawning
yet still strong and ready
for the next flight
they rest in the night
over their empty pockets
where their scales once were
and think of the fortune
they will soon again incur
perhaps the webs
were not traps at all
but paths to rid us
of the scales we no longer need
and we were caught
only for a moment so we could become
who we were meant to be.

# Jesus In Brooklyn

I found Jesus in Brooklyn
just a little past Nooklyn
where they slung studios
In a hipster sweater
despite the weather
It's burning up in here
because my soul is on FIRE.
Do you hear your daughter?
you did and you will
BRING on the water.
I found Jesus in Brooklyn
heart broken and full of spackle
it was time not to mend but to REMAKE
in this colorful tabernacle.
I saw red dresses and Easter hats
shiny shoes and faded tats
they were a motley crew
soul tugging
love chugging
inviting me
to drink up too.
Your mercy bottle never dries up.
I found Jesus in Brooklyn
and he said
*You are enough.*

# Sidewalk

I'll take the cracks in the sidewalk
where the weeds grow and dreams go
to think about life
for a while.
I'll take the bottles on the curb
looking for a place
to erase
the pain they've caused.
I'll take the sun
as it warms the asphalt
that holds me up
and you down
it takes us where
we need to go
even if we never get there
at least
we had the sidewalk
a place to talk
and wonder
under an umbrella
hoping for thunder.

# Sunflowers

I found them in Paris
whispering quietly on the ground
and he scooped them up
with his eyes on a vase
but surely sunflowers
are not meant to be contained?
anymore than they are meant to be
scattered to and fro
a truth told time and again
by one Van Gogh
Surely they were born for the sun
to spread their arms
in worship and delight
a kaleidoscope of saffron
to soften the night
They know just how many moments
to dance in the sun
before they face east
Perhaps I could learn from them
and not be so bound by the heat
and the fear of being alone
Perhaps a beautifully made vase
molded and fired by a loving hand
would make a happy home.

# Libra

You are the scales
and yet you carry them
until you break them
for a better way.
Rules are meant
to be glided upon
and divided into
equal pieces
that you can fit
in your pocket just right.
You are the day
and you are the night
and you detest them both with wild
delight.
You know how many
thousands
of shades of gray there are
But lack the patience of mind
to explain
exactly what they are
to someone
wasting the sublime
and wishing upon a star.
The time is now
until it was yesterday
you can read all the hands of the
clock
even the ones between
work and play
an outlier, you are both
the water and the fire
you are the oxygen
people need
and yet your lover
must sometimes
remind you to breathe.
The levies are going out

and the seeds
are sprouting
you are the whisper
at the end of the wind
but also the shouting.
Some will love you
and others
will plug their nose
and find you
a bitter pill, perhaps they are
genetically predisposed.
Some will not
some will
there must be a reason
a season
for the falling of their leaves
the rolling of their sleeves
no one just believes
except you
when you pour a glass of infinity
And can't get enough.

# Harvest Moon

My driveway is cracked
down the center
and to the end, still
roots protruding
hope alluding
you always said
she was a friend.
The pines are uprooting and chaos
is looting
the quiet corners
of my mind
and the sap is sticky
and oh so tricky
but this moment
is still mine.
Your fire is bright, like Apollo
and I hope I have the fight
to follow the path you started
tending the garden
you imparted
I shall pour the water
for the thirsty and willing
and warm the chilling
that you once had
in your  bone
I am comforted
to see you there
home.
Tucked in peace and rapture
It stirs me
as the image lured me
I took out my phone
to see if the sky could be tamed
but not even an Apple could handle
the zenith's appetite.
For your light
was not
ours to capture

only to remember
and so I felt
you on my skin
like I did earlier today and
suddenly
It all made sense.

# If I am Free

If I am
then I am also …..not
If I am free
then I am also….caught
If I am alone
then I am also together
with the lonely.
If I am at home
it is only
because I've been without one.

If I am my bones
I am also the spaces
in between.
If I am the quiet
I'm also deep inside my scream.

If am my story
I am also every word
I never wrote
If am the wheel
then I am also the road
as the dust
kissed the spoke.

If I am a soft dream dancing
then I am also my fears romancing
If am the branch
then I am also the wind
that blows it away.

# Alchemy

From the little pigeon river
to the clingmans dome
you're always climbing
trying to understand your home
whether in your hands
or in your heart
always putting magic together
and then pulling it apart
holding each piece with reverie
like a kid that caught a firefly
in the summer symphony
you're always chasing
creation and her alchemy
from the breaking of the bread
to the rising of the dawn
with your hands dirty
and your heart worthy
for the chorus of every song
even your cells
want to strum along
from reason to rapture
it's the joy you're after.

# The Girl with Golden Hair

I met a pretty nymph
in the wake
of my last mistake
she had golden hair
shining
and flowers at her feet
she smelled of jasmine and grace
and offered me a place
off the ground
she brushed off the dirt looked me
in the eyes
and said, you are NOT your hurt
she said
I will believe for you
until you can
stop trying so hard
to understand
not every sum can be found
put down your pen
and lay your numbers down
she took me to the cave where
Helios played
and I felt the heat
and the hope
for a better day.
She held my hand
until I was ready
to let it go and watch
the chariot in the sky
and think about something  other
than you and I
she said
I will believe for you
until you can
stop trying to hard
to understand
Not every sum wants to be found
put down your pen

and lay your numbers down
they won't add up
if you try to put them in rows
stop watering your woes and take
these flowers instead
you can hold them
and love them
without your head
she said
I will believe for you
until you can.

# A Thousand Times

You saved my life
A thousand times
When you were knitted together
In my womb
And when you arrived
To warn me and to warm me
To cling to you
To sing to you to drown out
the noise
You reminded me
I had a voice.
You saved my life
A thousand times
When you tricked me
into self care
Sneaking in some rest
On the living room chair
So I could make it through
The days with you
Reaching
And hungering
For a life so grand
One you would take a part
A million times
So you could understand.
You saved my life
A thousand times
When you entertained us all
With your chicken dance
You enthralled me
with your delight
over the stories we read
Your first word, was not, "mama"
but "kitty" instead
from a book you could not
get enough of
what a pleasure it was to share
a common love.

You saved my life
A thousand times
with birthday parties
and jeans with no buttons
going to school
without a production
shoes without laces
no red now-or-laters
lots and lots of elevators
and driving on roads
outside my comfort zone
through a myriad of moving boxes
Your little half dimple
was always home.
You saved my life
A thousand times
with your scratchy writing and
your tongue
getting twisted
giving your candy away
and retelling
your Pokemon tales
in case we missed it.
with your looking back
for your sisters
and waiting for them to catch up
with your compassion
and curiosity
and disdain for mediocrity
with your creative jolts
and cheeky rhymes
you have held my heart
at least,
A thousand times.

# Couch Crashing

Two and a half feet, I think
Just enough to let daydreams
get the best of me
Soft enough to sleep
but too hard to think
and maybe that's why
her arms comforted me.
Just enough room
for someone else
when the TV is bad
and the moon is asleep
But not too cavernous
for fears to get the best of me.
It's the perfect perch
for a Big Sister, Door Locker
Part-time Helicopter
Everyone is home
the day is done.
You can't be alone
on a bed
made for one.

# Rock Climbing

I do not know if the rocks are numbered or not
or if the sliding fickle ones were saved for some,
while others travel from safe to sturdy and then stop.
I don't get to know, and perhaps that is best,
lest I berate myself so.
We climbed against the same clock
along the same cliffs, with spraying ocean foam,
only I left damp and she was soaked to the bone.
It doesn't seem fair that I get to keep climbing,
and she has to stop.
But I know she would grieve more, if I let my guilt
keep me from vista at the top.
So I will tarry forward, and so will she,
on a different plane.
and we will both find heaven,
if love has her way.

# Spilling my Purse

How much of this really mattered?
I asked myself with purse splattered
on the sidewalk, teasing the curb
pants gathered to meet the chalk
and prepare for the swerve
at the intersection
of what I want and what I need.
So I eyed it all carefully
and waited for my retina
and frontal lobe to play for me.
Sometimes the zipper
needs to do its work
and close us off from the junk
we don't deserve
ticket stubs and receipts
the remnants of tasty treats
now stale
cut outs and coupons of impulses
no longer for sale.
Earring backs
and a package of mints
almost gone
lint and the fits
she jumped on
wrappers and reasons and help
with the seasons in a bottle
I scavenged full throttle
and found words to a song
and a necklace I hoped
would someday belong.
So I spilled the contents
and took my chance
to find meaning in her dividends
For the teacher said
The great thing about things falling apart
is you can pick up the pieces
you really want.

"And still, after all this time, the
Sun has never said to the Earth

'You owe me.'

*Look what happens with love like
that. It lights up the sky."*

**- Rumi**

# My Word

What is my word?
This question has waged war under my skin
It washes over me
One moment and then evaporates into the air thin
ENOUGH!
I question whether I had it at all
What is my word??
That one that stretches me so
makes me dig deep
And look UP
drink the water
get my sleep
I tried a few, warrior, champion, even athlete…
In hopes my soul would meet
just the right sound
she had been searching for
laureate, composer, connector….
Should this word evoke epiphany
or does that require hustling more….I ask myself
pacing outside my shadow calling's door
Maybe I am being told no
because I am the one
born to scream YES!
The shoulds and should nots never got me anywhere
I will remind myself this
when I see SHAME curling up her fist
When I see pressure whispering to resistance
I will not join their game
I will only answer to my hearts' name
I shall not climb someone else's peak
For all this time
trying to be a Roman
And I was really Greek.

# Stones

Let them be what we walk on
to get to the other side
not what we throw and then hide.

Let them be what we build with
not what we kill with
let them be painted
and left for others to find
so that they know the world is kind.

Let them be collected
in a jar by a seven year old's bed
not resurrected for a penthouse
we will eventually dread.

Let them be born for
brick oven pies
for our nephews and nieces
and scrumptious bread
we can tear into pieces
while we share our stories
and heal our wounds.
Let the stones be for creating
not for our tombs.

# Passion Flower

She said she knew the type of flower I was
I did not belong in a vase.
I felt the warmth that wraps you
when someone sees you beyond your face
and I wondered how some people have that craft so honed
and others don't even try to give it a go
Some things, I am not meant to understand
so I leave the frustrations for the fighting
and go back to my climb
reaching for the sun
and for the very best view
to really see everyone
when they are not looking and posing
snapping and app-ing
out all the messy goodness
that makes them great
even the little flies
my tendrils accidentally ate
they had a purpose I am sure
If only to remind us that sometimes our praying arms
can also swat
the darkness away
and make room for the butterflies
and hummingbirds and bees
and all the other pollinators
looking to feast
I have room for them
the dream pushers and Do-Gooders
the way makers
and Life chasers
Bring them to me
and we shall drink my tea
and see God
when we fall asleep.

# Phoenix

She rose up hotter than July
and we followed her and didn't know why
like a fire that made room for the strong to grow
She held secrets in her fingertips
we all wanted to know
She broke bread with the Gods on Olympus
And love as her witness
said "Screw your plans"
I am here for the roots and the reckoning
And adventures I don't have to understand.

# Cat's Eye

I was holding a cat's eye in my hand
leaning in to her mystery
and hoping to understand
something soothing about her saffron and cinnamon tones
like coffee with the right amount of cream
and that lovely friend that makes you feel at home
I found myself pondering and wondering
how different she looked when the light
waltzed with her in a certain place
when I let her tumble through my fingers
and could see more of her face
We are just like that, aren't we?
Appearing to be one thing
but then so much more
after study of our layers and prisms
colors and -isms
and so we all are from the same rock
just packaged in different cuts
of quartz and dust.

# Looking for Light

I am an explorer
of the beyond
past time
past the constraints
of our mind.
I meet souls
way down deep
past the trees
in the Age of Aquarius
at zero degrees
Jupiter and Saturn
converge
just as the water does
in a pattern, already
prescribed
because we need meaning
we need a tribe
So in this moment
hungry for light
explorers
like me
will call it
the Christmas Star
and shall no longer
fear the night.

# Surrender

The flower bud closing at just the right time
to avoid the scorch
of the midday heat
hardly an heroic feat
True surrender my dear
is not loud and proud
or bothering anyone
but a daily act of knowing
when to step in
and out of the sun.

# A Gift To Give

You would remind us
that we don't always have to understand
But we can not sit down
when we were born to stand
when we are shown a path
the way to go
we can not pretend
we can not unknow.
Most suffering, if not all, is self-induced
But our God is a God of miracles
lest we get confused.

You would say
you are a gift to give
you are a sight to behold
you are mist on the morning lake
and magic to unfold
you are a gift to give
and a song to sing
the only one born
To stop your suffering.

# To Be Seen

There is no sweeter sound
to any man
than the sound of his own name
said Carnegie and his faithful gang
And there is no sweeter feeling
to an artist
when you ask her
about her canvas
How did her heart even start this?

To a musician
when you ask him
about his song
to a builder
when you ask about this home
to a writer
when you ask about what she wrote
to a sailor
when you ask about his boat.

When you see the things we care about
you see us
when you call them by their name
sweetly, you call us
perhaps, that is love.

# Hey Mamas (and Daddies)

Hey mamas, I see you
cryin' in the dollar aisle
leanin' on your red carts
and tryin' your best to smile.

Hey mamas, I see you
and I want to throw
my arms around you and SING
You are NOT alone
in my heart, you have a home.

Hey mamas, I see you
pretty nails and kitchen's dirty
I promise the shine of neither
make you worthy.

You are not, what you do
You are not, what you have
or what you prove
and you are not
what you outlast.

You are so much more
than the darkness of right now
and so much more than your past
Hey mamas I see you
and your Creator does too.

# Flowers In My Hair

If didn't care
I would put flowers in my hair instead of a vase
so I could take them with me
while I walk
and I would whisper to each stalk
Let's be fabulous today!
and love all the sinners
dance at the grocery
and say the wrong things
at fancy dinners.

If I didn't care
I would wear elastic everywhere
so I could bend and breathe
after too much cheese
and never give
a second thought
to YES, more please!

The chef would be delighted
to see his gift loved so much
no need to be so tough
he wouldn't have a care
instead he'd hurry home
to bring his wife
flowers
to put in her hair.

# A Way Is Being Made

Right now
this moment
a way is being made
in the desert
on the blacktop
in the gut of someone you cherish
in the street where you thought
you would surely perish.

Right now
a gaping hole
is craving to be filled
with goodness, with light
formidable matches
for our daily fright.

Right now
the old branches
have snapped off and the new ones
are being decorated with green
and the beauty is being seen
in the SUN and in your heart
the mastery is not done
but at its' very start
Right now
this moment
A way is being made
in the sand
in the gravel
in the bodies of those
with HOPE
that can not be unraveled
And so it is.

# I See God In Smooth And Smiling Bald Heads

I see God in backyard Magnolia trees
the neighbor's tomatoes
but also in the vines of Hafiz.

I see God in smooth and smiling, bald heads
In the Good News
and in biscuits
soaking up gravy dredge.

I see God in awkward questionsasked by nieces
and handmade threads that hug our tired pieces.

I see God in terracotta pots painted by loving hands
and friends that whisk us away
despite our plans.

I see God in the man, that helped
push my car off the road
and all his stories
untold.

# En Plein Air

What if, just for one day
we all lived in the plein air
and walked only as far
as we could carry our brushes?
What if we surrendered
to the light God rendered
and forgot our filters and our phones
and took a break
from our earthly homes?

What if, just for one day
we all breathed in the plein air
embraced the fragrance
that it gave us
and left behind
the potions and the notions
that we ever needed more
And we became
synergized
energized
walking away
RESTORED.

What if, just for one day
we all listened in the plein air
without the distractions and the contraptions
that kept us from hearing one another
that keep us from understanding
our sister, our brother.

What if, just for one day
we all loved in the plein air
like the leaves dance openly with the breeze
not caring who they please
like the child smiling at a stranger
there is no fear
there is no danger.

# Love is Talking

If there is a castle on a cloud
then there is a girl between the masks.
If there is a place in the sun
then there is a man between the tasks.
I've heard rumors of these things
in the quiet of the morning
harmonizing with the air conditioning
listen, she is whispering
like an excited child
she wants to tell you so
there is more than looking for "likes"
everywhere you go.
There is a picture she is scribbling
and asking your soul to render
Why must you fight the truth?
You know the power in surrender.
Ssh, tell fear to simmer down
love is talking, and she's walking
straight to you
grab her hand and meet her!
All you need is the openness to receive her.
Behold I stand at the door and knock.....
don't you remember that from Sunday school?
Ssh, you can not hear
if you are trying so hard to be cool!
If there is a girl between the masks
and a man between the tasks
there is a spirit our fear outlasts.
Love is talking, if we will listen

Divinity will persist
but our hearts must
be open for the bliss
for you can not hold a miracle
in a clenched fist.

# On This Day

On this day
right on it
sitting proudly
like the sun
on the shelf of the horizon
you said TA-DAH!
Here I am world
for you, a dream
with ten toes
a perfect girl.
Your only mission
was to love and to be loved
and that was enough
Your arms were made
for holding and your legs were made
for carrying your curiosity
into all the corners
you could
and you only knew
I WILL and hadn't yet learned "I Should"
On this day
my heart once again
jumped outside of itself
and held my hand.
And it didn't matter
that I couldn't understand
because love transcends all proofs
argued on mortal ground
what once was lost
was found
and the song
started writing itself
On this day
you set like the sun
on the earth's shelf.

# Fairy Tales

No wonder our little girls grow up wanting to be saved
for that is the only tape
for them, we have played
year after year of fairy tales have them held helpless
in towers and caves
overcome by witches, wolves and knaves
and so, I'm happy to see other stories
put out for them to buy
ones of capability
instead of waiting for magic in the sky.
What if their rides were not side saddle?
but full throttle into the forest?
And they could save themselves
and teach the dragons to adore us?
WITHOUT, a regent of the king
or an enchanted ring.
What if they did not wait for the sword
of their father or brother
but instead learned to weld
it from their mother?
Blessed are the meek
we are told.
Your husband is the one
ordained to be bold!
But for every hour
we are waiting
for someone to climb
the tower
that is another time
we could have built our own.

# Pretty Flo

Pretty Flo
does not worry
or hurry
she just does.
She lets her wonder
move her
to the next right step.
She does not fret
over what others might say
It is her night
It is her day.
She will put the moon in a basket
and carry it
as far as she likes
and she will wrap herself in the sun
whenever she feels
the whisper
of lonely nights.
Pretty Flo
does not believe in luck
she is luck on legs
and cares nothing
of turning heads.
She does not wait on a bench
waiting to be picked
she was not made
for the waiting
but for the making.

# Like a Crown

She just tore in here
screaming for sprinkles
for the top of her ice cream
But they had to be golden
so her ice cream could "wear a crown"
How could I say no to that?
I had to laugh
and acquiesce
despite her bedtime past
for surely a lovely metaphor
Is worth staying up for?

# No. 19 in C Major

Slow to start, but the most revered
proof that defying convention is not to be feared
An unnerving whisper
that invites the mind to listen
and says to the heart, "You are forgiven"
On paper we have a number, we have a name
It makes people feel comfortable
for us to be the same
but I know and you know
we are our spirits unbound by perfect or imperfect
soft or sharp and other limits
they gave us a name and then called us dissonance.
But is that such a terrible thing
to not be resolved
to not be tamed?
They say her power is the tension she causes
the lingering of the first movement
the soft subtle pauses
that cause our souls to strain
and our minds to stretch
Isn't that where beauty unfolds
in places we least suspect?
What was at first harsh
is not harsh anymore?
As the second phase comes
to throw expectation out the door
Allegro!
Our fears, we must let go
so we can be suspended into the resolve
that has been calling us in
Faster and stronger
as our bouts of surrender are longer
until we let the fiery strings
transport us to another place
not of here, but here all at once
nor Mozart or magic can be ruled by consonance
For love
Is not efficient.

# Consolation

Consolation
that word got a bad rap
and that was not her intent
like a beautiful dress
ruined by a smokey bar
Is this what I shaved my legs for?

Consolation
I know you are a sweet girl it is
hidden in your handwriting
I see now that expectation
has drifted away
No more listening to what the neighbors say
to be present is a wonderful gift.

Consolation
Is not a dirty word
third is not less than the first
if it honors what you deserve
showing up is half the game
and that's something worth
celebrating
Halftime shows and tailgating
whatever makes you feel
bigger than yourself,
and
not
so
alone.

# One More Lap

It is not the darkness
that hurts so  much
It's the space between
that is so tough
the vast space
In the going
back and forth
the fear that
you don't have another
lap in you.

# Havasu

What do you mean?
You're building a road
through here?
How will we drink?
How will we eat?
Will our name cease to mean
the people of the blue-green waters
that once were ours
But now, no longer for
our sons and daughters.
Our feet were not meant
for this pavement you are putting in
They are meant for the earth, the dust, the dirt
for grounding
in the rhapsody of spirit
which you seek to hurt
in the name of beauty
which is already here.
How can you capture something
that is already yours?
We must lean into this fear
that is moving us, changing
the home, we have always known
I must trust that a bridge will be made
even if it's generations later
by a judge
we never met.
We must not quit
We must not fret
We will not cry
We will not beg
for we know we cannot
feel the life blood of this canyon
without going, a little close to the edge.